John Boyle O'Reilly

The Statues in the Block, and Other Poems

John Boyle O´Reilly

The Statues in the Block, and Other Poems

ISBN/EAN: 9783337373467

Printed in Europe, USA, Canada, Australia, Japan

Cover: Foto ©Thomas Meinert / pixelio.de

More available books at **www.hansebooks.com**

THE

STATUES IN THE BLOCK,

AND OTHER POEMS.

BY

JOHN BOYLE O'REILLY.

SECOND EDITION.

BOSTON:
ROBERTS BROTHERS.
1881.

881,

O'Reilly.

RESS:

N, Cambridge.

TO

THE MEMORY OF ELIZA BOYLE,

My Mother.

CONTENTS.

———◆———

POEMS.

Life is a certainty,

    Death is a doubt;

Men may be dead

    While they're walking about.

Love is as needful

    To being as breath;

Loving is dreaming, —

    And waking is death.

THE STATUES IN THE BLOCK.

"LOVE is the secret of the world," he said;
      "The cup we drain and still desire to drink.
The loadstone hungers for the steel; the steel,
Inert amid a million stones, responds to this.
So yearn and answer hearts that truly love:
Once touch their life-spring, it vibrates to death;
And twain athrill as one are nature-wed."

But silent stood the three who heard, nor smiled
Nor looked agreement.   Strangers these who stood
Within a Roman studio — still young,
But sobered each with that which follows joy
At life's fresh forenoon, and the eye of each

Held deep within a restless eager light,

As gleams a diamond in a darkened room

With radiance hoarded from the vanished sun.

" The meteor-stone is dense and dark in space,

But bursts in flame when through the air it rushes ;

And our dull life is like an aerolite

That leaps to fire within the sphere of love."

Unchecked his mood ran on : " Sweet amorous hours

That lie in years as isles in tropic seas,

You spring to view as Art is born of Love,

And shape rich beauties in this marble block ! "

Before them rose within the shaded light

A tall and shapely mass of Alp-white crystal

Fresh from the heart of a Carrara quarry.

" Opaque to you this marble ; but to me,

Whose eyes the chrism of passion has anointed,

The stone is pregnant with a life of love.

Within this monolith there lives a form

Which I can see and would reveal to you,

Could hand and chisel swiftly follow sight.

From brow to foot her lissome form stands forth —

The ripe lips smiling reached ; with nestling press,

As round the sailor frozen in the berg

The clear ice closes on the still dead face,

The marble, grown translucent, touches soft

Each comely feature — rippled hair, and chin,

And lily sweep of bust and hip and limb —

Ah, sweet mouth pouting for the lips that cling,

And white arms raised all quivering to the clasp —

Ah, rich throat made for burning lover's kiss,

And reckless bodice open to the swell,

And deep eyes soft with love's suffusion — Love !

O Love ! still living, memory and hope,

Beyond all sweets thy bosom, breath, and lips —

My jewel and the jewel of the world ! "

They stood in silence, each one rapt and still,

As if the lovely form were theirs as his,

Till one began — harsh voice and clouded face —

With other presence in his eye — and said :

" Opaque to me with such a glow-worm ray

As Love's torch flings — but, mark, the dense rock

    melts .

When from my soul on fire the fiercer beam,

The mighty calcium-glare of hate leaps out

And eats the circumambient marble — See !

Laid bare as corpse to keen anatomist,

With every sinuous muscle picked with shadow,

And every feature tense with livid passion,

And all the frame aheave with sanguine throbs —

The ecstasy of agonized Revenge !

O stone, reveal it — how my parting kiss

Was wet upon her mouth when other lips

Drank deep the cursèd fountain ; how the coin

I hung with rapture 'tween her glowing breasts,

And fondly thought if I should die and she

Should live till age had blanched her hair and flesh,

This golden medal's touch would still have power

To light the love-fire in the faded eyes

And swell the shrivelled breast to maiden roundness —

This thought I nursed — O Stygian abyss ! —

Away thy picture of the rippled hair !

Her hair was rippled and her eyes were deep,

Her breasts and limbs were white and lily-curved,

But all the woman, soul and wondrous flesh,

Was poison-steeped and veined with vicious fire ;

And I, blind fool who trusted, was but one

Who swooned with love beside her — But I drank

The wine she filled, and made her eat the dregs —

I drenched her honey with my sea of gall.

I see her in the marble where she shrinks

In shuddered fear, as if my face were fire —

Her cowering shadow making whiter still

The face of him that writhes beside her feet.

I see him breathe, the last deep breath, and turn

His eyes upon me horror-filled — his hand,

Still hot with wanton dalliance, clutched hard

Across the burning murder in his side —

And now he sinks still glaring — And my heart

Is there between them, petrified, O God !

And pierced by that red blow that struck their guilt.

O balm and torture ! he must hate who loves,

And bleed who strikes to see thy face, Revenge ! "

Grown deep the silence for the words that died,

And paler still the marble for its grief.

" Ah, myrrh and honey ! " spake a third, whose eyes

Were deep with sorrow for the woe ; " blind hands

That grope for flowers and pierce the flesh with thorns !

All love of woman still may turn to hate,

As wine to bitterness, as noon to night.

But sweeter far and deeper than the love

Of flesh for flesh, is the strong bond of hearts

For suffering Motherland — to make her free !

Love's joy is short, and Hate's black triumph bitter,

And loves and hates are selfish — save for thee,

THE STATUES IN THE BLOCK.

O chained and weeping at thy pillar's foot,

Thy white flesh eaten by accursèd bands.

No love but thine can satisfy the heart,

For love of thee holds in it hate of wrong,

And shapes the hope that moulds humanity !

Not mine your passions, yet I weigh them well —

Who loves a greater sinks all lesser love,

Who hates a tyrant loses lesser hate.

My Land ! I see thee in the marble, bowed

Before thy tyrant, bound at foot and wrist —

Thy garments rent — thy wounded shoulder bare —

Thy chained hand raised to ward the cruel blow —

My poor love round thee scarf-like, weak to hide

And powerless to shield thee — but a boy

I wound it round thee, dearest, and a man

I drew it close and kissed thee — Mother, wife !

For thee the past and future days ; for thee

The will to trample wrong and strike for slaves ;

For thee the hope that ere mine arm be weak

And ere my heart be dry may close the strife

In which thy colors shall be borne through fire,
And all thy griefs washed out in manly blood —
And I shall see thee crowned and bound with love,
Thy strong sons round thee guarding thee.   O star
That lightens desolation, o'er her beam,
Nor let the shadow of the pillar sink
Too deep within her, till the dawn is red
Of that white noon when men shall call her Queen ! "

The deep voice quivering with affection ceased,
And silent each they saw within the stone
The captive nation and the mother's woe.
Yet while their hearts the fine emotion warmed,
Ere ebbed the deep-pulsed throb of brotherhood,
The last one spoke, and held the wave at full : —

" Yea, brothers, his the noblest for its grief ;
Your love was loss — but his was sacrifice.
Your light was sunlight, for the shallow sense,

That bends the eyes on earth and thinks it sees ;

His love was nightlike, when we see the stars,

Forgetting petty things around our feet.

Yet here, too, find his weakness, for his hope

Is still for sunlight, and your shallow sense,

And golden crowns and queendom for his love.

I, too, within the stone behold a statue,

Far less than yours, but greater, for I know

My symbol a beginning, not an end.

O, Grief, with Hope !   The marble fades — behold !

The little hands still crossed — a child in death.

My link with love — my dying gift from her

Whose last look smiled on both, when I was left

A loveless man, save this poor gift, alone.

My heart had wound its tendrils round one life,

But, when my joy was deepest, she was stricken,

And I was powerless to save.   My prayers

And piteous cries were flung against my face —

My life was blighted by the curse of Heaven !

But from the depths her love returned to soothe :

Her dear hand reached from death and placed her
    child

Where she had lived, within the riven tendrils,

And firmly these closed round their second treasure.

And she, my new love, in her infant hold

Took every heart-string as her mother's gift,

And touched such tender fine-strung chords, and
    played

Such music in my heart as filled my life

With trembling joy and fondness for the child.

I feared to be so blest — her baby cheek,

When laid on mine, was Heaven's sweetest touch ;

And when she looked me in the eyes, I saw

Her mother look at me from deep within,

And bless me for the love I gave and won.

Yet, when I loved her most she, too, was doomed :

I saw it come upon her like a shadow,

And watched the change, appalled at first, but set

To ward the danger from my darling. She,

As day by day still failing, grew so tender

And crept so often to my heart, as if,

'Though but a babe who could not speak a word,

She knew full well my life would soon be shattered.

But all my love was fruitless, and my prayers

To leave her with me beat the gates in vain.

I thought my love must hold her, till at last

I held the tiny body like a leaf

All day and night within my arms ; and so,

Close nestled to my yearning heart, Death passed,

As merciless as God, but left that look

Of two dead loves, as if Death's self knew pity.

And I was lost heart-withered in a night

That knew no star and held no ray of hope,

And heard no word but my despairing curse

With lifted hands, at life and Him who gave it !

My graves were all I had — the little mound

Where my hands laid her, with the sweet young

      grass —

The tiny hill that grew until the sun

Was hid behind it, and I sat below

And gnawed my heart in grief within its shadow.

So one day bowed in woe beside the grave

The weight grew deadly, and I called aloud

That God should witness to my life in ruin.

And God's word reached me through the little grave

Where in the grass my face was buried weeping —

His peace came through it like a pent-up breath

That rolled from some great world whose gates had

      oped,

And blew upon my wild and hardened heart,

And swept my woe before it like a leaf.

My dried heart drank the meaning of the peace :

True love shall trust, and selfish love must die,

For trust is peace, and self is full of pain ;

Arise, and heal thy brother's grief ; his tears

Shall wash thy love and it will live again.

O little grave, I thought 't was love had died,

But in thy bosom only lies my sorrow.

I see my darling in the marble now —

My wasted leaf — her kind eyes smiling fondly,

And through her eyes I see the love beyond,

The biding light that moves not — and I know

That when God gives to us the clearest sight

He does not touch our eyes with Love, but Sorrow."

THE FAME OF THE CITY.

A GREAT rich city of power and pride,
  With streets full of traders, and ships on the tide ;
With rich men and workmen and judges and preachers,
The shops full of skill and the schools full of teachers.

The people were proud of their opulent town :
The rich men spent millions to bring it renown ;
The strong men built and the tradesmen planned ;
The shipmen sailed to every land ;
The lawyers argued, the schoolmen taught,
And a poor shy Poet his verses brought,
And cast them into the splendid store.

The tradesmen stared at his useless craft ;
The rich men sneered and the strong men laughed ;

The preachers said it was worthless quite ;

The schoolmen claimed it was theirs to write ;

But the songs were spared, though they added nought

To the profit and praise the people sought,

That was wafted at last from distant climes ;

And the townsmen said : " To remotest times

We shall send our name and our greatness down ! "

The boast came true ; but the famous town

Had a lesson to learn when all was told :

The nations that honored cared nought for its gold,

Its skill they exceeded an hundred-fold ;

It had only been one of a thousand more,

Had the songs of the Poet been lost to its store.

Then the rich men and tradesmen and schoolmen said

They had never derided, but praised instead ;

And they boast of the Poet their town has bred.

HEART–HUNGER.

THERE is no truth in faces, save in children :
    They laugh and frown and weep from nature's
      keys ;
But we who meet the world give out false notes,
The true note dying muffled in the heart.

O, there be woful prayers and piteous wailing,
That spirits hear, from lives that starve for love !
The body's food is bread ; and wretches' cries
Are heard and answered : but the spirit's food
Is love ; and hearts that starve may die in agony
And no physician mark the cause of death.

You cannot read the faces ; they are masks, —
Like yonder woman, smiling at the lips,

Silk-clad, bejewelled, lapped with luxury,

And beautiful and young — ay, smiling at the lips,

But never in the eyes from inner light :

A gracious temple hung with flowers without —

Within, a naked corpse upon the stones !

O, years and years ago the hunger came —

The desert-thirst for love — she prayed for love —

She cried out in the night-time of her soul for love !

The cup they gave was poison whipped to froth.

For years she drank it, knowing it for death ;

She shrieked in soul against it, but must drink :

The skies were dumb — she dared not swoon or
      scream.

As Indian mothers see babes die for food,

She watched dry-eyed beside her starving heart,

And only sobbed in secret for its gasps,

And only raved one wild hour when it died !

O Pain, have pity ! Numb her quivering sense ;

O Fame, bring guerdon ! Thrice a thousand years

Thy boy-thief with the fox beneath his cloak

Has let it gnaw his side unmoved, and held the world ;

And she, a slight woman, smiling at the lips,

With repartee and jest — a corpse-heart in her breast !

MULEY MALEK, THE KING.

THUNDER of guns, and cries — banners and
    spears and blood !
Troops have died where they stood holding the
    vantage points —
They have raced like waves at a wall, and dashed
    themselves to death.

Dawn the fight begin, and noon was red with its noon.
The armies stretch afar — and the plain of Alcazar
Is drenched with Moorish blood.

On one side, Muley the King — Muley Malek the
    Strong.
He had seized the Moorish crown because it would fit
    his brows.
Hamet the Fair was king ; but Muley pulled him
    down, because he was strong.

The fierce sun glares on the clouds of dust and battle
    smoke,
The hoarsened soldiers choke in the blinding heat.
Muley the King is afield, but sick to the death.
Borne on a litter he lies, his blood on fire, his eyes
Flaming with fever light.
Hamah Tabah the Captain, stands by the curtained bed,
Telling him news of the fight — how the waves roll and
    rise, and clash and mingle and seethe.
And Hamah bends to the scene. He peers under
    archéd hand —
As an eagle he stoops to the field.   One hand on the hilt
Is white at the knuckles, so fiercely gripped ; while
    the hand
That had parted the curtains before now clutches the
    silk and wrings.

Hamet's squadrons are moving in mass — their lines
    are circling the plain !
The thousands of Muley stand, like bison dazed by
    an earthquake ;

They are stunned by the thud of the fight, they are
       deer without a leader ;

Their charge has died like the impulse of missiles freed
       from the sling ;

Their spears waver like shaken barley, — they are
       dumb-struck and ready to fly !

Hamah Tabah the Captain, in words like the pouring
       of pitch, has painted

The terrible scene for the sick King, and terrible
       answer follows.

Up from the couch of pain, disdaining the bonds of
       weakness ;

Flinging aside disease as a wrestler flings his tunic ;

Strong with the smothered fire of fever, and fiercer
       far than its flaming,

Rises in mail from the litter Muley Malek the King !

Down on his plunging stallion, in the eyes of the shud-
       dered troops,

His bent plume like a smoke, and his sword like a flame,

Smelting their souls with his courage, he rides before
    his soldiers !

They bend from his face like the sun — their eyes are
    blind with shame —

They thrill as a stricken tiger thrills, gathering his limbs
    from a blow ;

They raise their faces, and watch him, sworded and
    mailed and strong ;

They watch him, and shout his name fiercely — "*Muley, the King !*"

Grimly they close their ranks, drinking his face like
    wine ;

Strength to the arm and wrath to the soul, and power —

Fuel and fire he was — and the battle roared like a
    crater !

Back to the litter, his face turned from the lines, and
    fixed

In a stare like the faces in granite, the King

Rode straight and strong, holding his sword

Soldierly, gripped on the thigh, grim as a king in iron !

Stiff in the saddle, stark, frowning — one hand is raised,

The mailéd finger is laid on the mouth :

" *Silence !* " the warning said to Hamah Tabah the
      Captain.

Help from his horse they give, moving him, still un-
      bending,

Down to the bed, and lay him within the curtains.

Mutely they answer his frown, like ridges of bronze,
      and sternly

Again is the mailed hand raised and laid on the lips
      in warning :

" *Silence !* " it said, and the meaning smote through
      their blood like flame,

As the tremor passed through his armor and the gray-
      ness crept o'er his features —

Muley the King was dead !

Furious the struggle and long, the armies with* teeth
aclench

And dripping weapons shortened, like athletes whose
blows have killed pain.

The soldiers of Hamet were flushed — but the spirit of
Muley opposed them ;

The weak of Muley grew strong when they looked at
the curtained litter.

Their thought of the King was wine in the thirst of
the fight ;

They saw that Hamah was there, still bending over the
bed ;

Holding the curtains wide and taking the order that
came

From the burning lips of the King, and sending it
down to his soldiers ;

They knew that Hamah the Captain was telling him
of the onset,

How they swept like hail on the fields, and left them
like sickled grain.

Back, as the waves in a tempest are flung from a cliff
    and scattered,

Burst and horribly broken and driven beneath with
    the impact,

Shivered, for once and forever, the conquered forces;
    King Hamet

Was slain by the sword, and the foreign monarch who
    helped him,

And the plain was swept by the besom of death:

There never was grander faith in a king!

Trophies and victors' crowns, bring them to bind his
    brow!

Circle his curtained bed — thousands and thousands,
    come!

It will cure him, and kill his pain — we must see him
    to-night again:

One glance of his love and pride for all the hosts that
    died —

To his bedside — come!

Rigid, with frowning brow, his finger laid on his lips,

They saw him — saw him and knew, and read the
   word that he spake,

Stronger than death, and they stood in their tears,
   and were silent,

Obeying the King !

REMORSE.

I REMEMBER when I was a boy
  That a grown girl wanted to kiss me ;
And I struggled, was angry, and shy,
  And ran off when she tried to caress me.

And I 've thought of that day through the years ;
  (What a moral, my friend, lies in this !)
Under every sweet leaf that appears
  Lurks a pain for the loss of that kiss.

The Infinite always is silent;
  It is only the Finite speaks.
Our words are the idle wave-caps
  On the deep that never breaks.
We may question with wand of science,
  Explain, decide, and discuss;
But only in meditation
  The Mystery speaks to us.

FROM THE EARTH, A CRY.

" The Years of Our Lord " 1870 to 1880. — The Rulers of Prussia and France make War. — The Paris Commune. — War for Rome between the Pope and the King of Italy. — War between Russia and Turkey. — England devastates Abyssinia, Ashantee, and Zululand. — One English Viceroy in India murdered. Another shot at. — Socialists attempt to kill the Emperor of Germany. — Internationalists fire at the King of Italy. — Nihilists thrice attempt to destroy the Czar. — The Mines of Siberia filled with Political Prisoners. — The Farmers of Ireland rebel in Despair against Rack-rents. — The Workmen of England emigrating from Starvation. — The Land of England, Scotland, and Ireland held by less than a Quarter of a Million of Men. — The Pittsburg Riots. — The American Strikes. — The End of the Decade.

CAN the earth have a voice? Can the clods have
  speech,
To murmur and rail at the demigods?
Trample them! Grind their vulgar faces in the clay!

The earth was made for lords and the makers of law;
For the conquerors and the social priests;

For traders who feed on and foster the complex
    life ;
For the shrewd and the selfish who plan and keep ;
For the heirs who squander the hoard that bears
The face of the king, and the blood of the serf,
And the curse of the darkened souls !

O Christ ! and O Christ ! In thy name the law !
In thy mouth the mandate ! In thy loving hand the
    whip !
They have taken thee down from thy cross and sent
    thee to scourge the people ;
They have shod thy feet with spikes and jointed thy
    dead knees with iron,
And pushed thee, hiding behind, to trample the poor
    dumb faces !

The spheres make music in space. They swing
Like fiery cherubim on their paths, circling their
    suns,

Mysterious, weaving the irrevealable,

Full of the peace of unity — sphere and its life at
    one —

Humming their lives of love through the limitless waste
    of creation.

God ! thou hast made man a test of Thyself !

Thou hast set in him a heart that bleeds at the cry of
    the helpless :

Through Thine infinite seas one world rolls silent,

Moaning at times with quivers and fissures of blood ;

Divided, unhappy, accursèd ; the lower life good,

But the higher life wasted and split, like grain with a
    cankered root.

Is there health in thy gift of life, Almighty ?

Is there grief or compassion anywhere for the poor ?

If these be, there is guerdon for those who hate the
    wrong

And leap naked on the spears, that blood may cry

For truth to come, and pity, and Thy peace.

The human sea is frozen like a swamp; and the kings
And the heirs and the owners ride on the ice and
  laugh.
Their war-forces, orders, and laws are the crusted field
  of a crater,
And they stamp on the fearful rind, deriding its flesh-
  like shudder.

Lightning! the air is split, the crater bursts, and the
  breathing
Of those below is the fume and fire of hatred.
The thrones are stayed with the courage of shotted
  guns.   The warning dies.
But queens are dragged to the block, and the knife of
  the guillotine sinks
In the garbage of pampered flesh that gluts its bed and
  its hinges.

Silence again, and sunshine.   The gaping lips are
  closed on the crater.

The dead are below, and the landless, and those who
　　live to labor

And grind forever in gloom that the privileged few
　　may live.

But the silence is sullen, not restful. It heaves like a
　　sea, and frets,

And beats at the roof till it finds another vent for its
　　fury.

Again the valve is burst and the pitch-cloud rushes, —
　　the old seam rends anew —

Where the kings were killed before, their names are
　　hewed from the granite —

Paris, mad hope of the slave-shops, flames to the
　　petroleuse !

Tiger that tasted blood — Paris that tasted freedom !

Never, while steel is cheap and sharp, shall thy king-
　　lings sleep without dreaming —

Never, while souls have flame, shall their palaces
　　crush the hovels.

Insects and vermin, ye, the starving and dangerous
    myriads,

List to the murmur that grows and growls ! Come
    from your mines and mills,

Pale-faced girls and women with ragged and hard-eyed
    children,

Pour from your dens of toil and filth, out to the air of
    heaven —

Breathe it deep, and hearken ! A Cry from the cloud
    or beyond it,

A Cry to the toilers to rise, to be high as the highest
    that rules them,

To own the earth in their lifetime and hand it down
    to their children !

Emperors, stand to the bar ! Chancellors, halt at the
    barracks !

Landlords and Lawlords and Tradelords, the spectres
    you conjured have risen —

Communists, Socialists, Nihilists, Rent-rebels, Strikers,
    behold !

They are fruit of the seed you have sown — God has
    prospered your planting. They come

From the earth, like the army of death. You have
    sowed the teeth of the dragon !

Hark to the bay of the leader ! You shall hear the
    roar of the pack

As sure as the stream goes seaward. The crust on
    the crater beneath you

Shall crack and crumble and sink, with your laws and
    rules

That breed the million to toil for the luxury of the
    ten —

That grind the rent from the tiller's blood for drones
    to spend —

That hold the teeming planet as a garden plot for a
    thousand —

That draw the crowds to the cities from the healthful
    fields and woods —

That copulate with greed and beget disease and
    crime —

That join these two and their offspring, till the world
    is filled with fear,

And falsehood wins from truth, and the vile and cun-
    ning succeed,

And manhood and love are dwarfed, and virtue and
    friendship sick,

And the law of Christ is a cloak for the corpse that
    stands for Justice !

— As sure as the Spirit of God is Truth, this Truth
    shall reign,

And the trees and lowly brutes shall cease to be higher
    than men.

God purifies slowly by peace, but urgently by fire.

PROMETHEUS — CHRIST.

LASHED to the planet, glaring at the sky,
   An eagle at his heart — the Pagan Christ !

Why is it, Mystery?   O, dumb Darkness, why
Have always men, with loving hearts themselves,
Made devils of their gods ?

                              The whirling globe
Bears round man's sweating agony of blood,
That Might may gloat above impotent Pain !

Man's soul is dual — he is half a fiend,
And from himself he typifies Almighty.

O, poison-doubt, the answer holds no peace :
Man did not make himself a fiend, but God.

Between them, what?   Prometheus stares
Through ether to the lurid eyes of Jove —
Between them, Darkness !

                              But the gods are dead —
Ay, Zeus is dead, and all the gods but Doubt,
And Doubt is brother devil to Despair !

What, then, for us?   Better Prometheus' fate,
Who dared the gods, than insect unbelief —
Better Doubt's fitful flame than abject nothingness !

O, world around us, glory of the spheres !
God speaks in ordered harmony — behold !
Between us and the Darkness, clad in light, —
Between us and the curtain of the Vast, — two Forms,
And each is crowned eternally — and One

Is crowned with flowers and tender leaves and grass,

And smiles benignly; and the other One,

With sadly pitying eyes, is crowned with thorns:

O Nature, and O Christ, for men to love

And seek and live by — Thine the dual reign —

The health and hope and happiness of men!

Behold our faith and fruit!——

What demon laughs?

Behold our books, our schools, our states,

Where Christ and Nature are the daily word;

Behold our dealings between man and man,

Our laws for home, our treaties for abroad;

Behold our honor, honesty, and freedom,

And, last, our brotherhood!   For we are born

In Christian times and ruled by Christian rules!

Bah!   God is mild, or he would strike the world

As men should smite a liar on the mouth.

Shame on the falsehood !   Let us tell the truth —
Nor Christ nor Nature rules, but Greed and Creed
And Caste and Cant and Craft and Ignorance.
Down to the dust with every decent face,
And whisper there the lies we daily live.
O, God forgive us !   Nature never can ;
For one is merciful, the other just.

Let us confess : by Nations first — our lines
Are writ in blood and rapine and revenge ;
Conquest and pride have motive been and law —
Christ walks with us to hourly crucifixion !

As Men ?   Would God the better tale were here :
Atom as whole, corruption, shrewdness, self.
Freedom ?   A juggle — hundreds slave for one, —
That one is free, and boasts, and lo ! the shame,
The hundreds at the wheel go boasting too.
Justice ?   The selfish only can succeed ;
Success means power — did Christ mean it so ? —

And power must be guarded by the law,

And preachers preach that law must be obeyed,

Ay, even when Right is ironed in the dock,

And Rapine sits in ermine on the bench !

Mercy ? Behold it in the reeking slums

That grow like cancers from the palace wall ;

Go hear it from the conquered — how their blood

Is weighed in drops, and purchased, blood for gold ;

Go ask the toiling tenant why he paid

The landlord's rent and let his children starve ;

Go find the thief, whose father was a thief,

And ask what Christian leech has cured his sin?

H·nesty ? Our law of life is Gain —

We must get gold or be accounted fools ;

The lovable, the generous, must be crushed

And substituted by the hard and shrewd.

What is it, Christ, this thing called Christian life,

Where Christ is not, where ninety slave for ten,

And never own a flower save when they steal it,

And never hear a bird save when they cage it?

Is this the freedom of Thy truth? Ah, woe

For those who see a higher, nobler law

Than his, the Crucified, if this be so !

O, man's blind hope — Prometheus, thine the gift —

That bids him live when reason bids him die !

We cling to this, as sailors to a spar —

We see that this is Truth : that men are one,

Nor king nor slave among them save by law ;

We see that law is crime, save God's sweet code

That laps the world in freedom : trees and men

And every life around us, days and seasons,

All for their natural order on the planet,

To live their lives, an hour, a hundred years,

Equal, content, and free — nor curse their souls

With trade's malign unrest, with books that breed

Disparity, contempt for those who cannot read ;

With cities full of toil and sin and sorrow,

Climbing the devil-builded hill called Progress !

Prometheus, we reject thy gifts for Christ's !

Selfish and hard were thine ; but His are sweet —

" Sell what thou hast and give it to the poor ! "

Him we must follow to the great Commune,

Reading his book of Nature, growing wise

As planet-men, who own the earth, and pass ;

Him we must follow till foul Cant and Caste

Die like disease, and Mankind, freed at last,

Tramples the complex life and laws and limits

That stand between all living things.and Freedom !

" *You gave me the key of your heart, my love ; .*

    Then why do you make me knock ? "

" *O, that was yesterday, Saints above !*

    , And last night — I changed the lock ! "

THE TEMPLE OF FRIENDSHIP.

IN the depths of the silent wood the temple of
　　Friendship stood,
Like a dream of snow-white stone, or a vestal all alone,
　　Undraped beside a stream.

The pious from every clime came there to rest for a
　　time,
With incense and gifts and prayer; and the stainless
　　marble stair
　　Was worn by fervent knees.

And everywhere the fame of the beautiful temple came,
With its altar white and pure, and its worship to allure
　　From gods that bring unrest.

The goddess was there to assuage (for this was the
    Golden Age)
The trials of all who staid and trustingly tried and
    prayed
      For the perfect grace.

Soldier and clerk and dame in couples and companies
    came ;
There were few who rode alone, for none feared the
    other one,
      So placid and safe the creed.

There came from afar one day, with a suite in rich
    array,
A lady of beauty rare, who bent to the plaintive air
      A handsome minstrel sung.

Her face was as calm and cold as the stamp of a queen
    on gold,
And the song the poet sung to a restful theme was
    strung,
      A tranquil air of peace.

But, as they happily rode to the holy and white abode,
They were watched from a cloud above by the mis-
chievous god of Love,
Who envied Friendship's reign.

They dreamt not of danger near, and their hearts felt
no shade of fear,
As they laid their rich offerings of flowers and precious
things
At Friendship's lovely feet.

They lingered long near the shrine, in the air of its
peace divine ;
By the shadowed stream they strayed, where often the
heavenly maid
Would smile upon their rest.

One day, with her white robe flown, she passed like a
dream alone,
Where they sat in a converse sweet, with the silver
stream at their feet
As still and as wise as they.

To the innermost temple's room, to the couch, and the
sacred loom

Where she weaves her placid will, the goddess came,
smiling still,

Unrobing for blissful rest.

[old,

O lily of perfect mould, the world had grown young, not

Had it bowed at thy milk-white feet with a love not
of fire, but heat, —

Sweet lotus of soft repose !

Like the moon her body glows, like the sun-flushed
Alpine snows ;

Her arms 'neath her radiant head, she sleeps, and lo !
o'er her bed

The wicked Cupid leans.

Even he cannot fly the feast which nor vestal nor
hoary priest

Had ever enjoyed before.   But, stealing her robe from
the floor,

He dons it and is gone.

By the stream, in the silent shade, he walks where
the two have made
Their resting-place for the noon : " 'T is Friendship ! "
they cry ; and soon
Love's guile on their hearts is laid.

" O, the goddess is good ! " she said, as she bent her
golden head
And looked in the minstrel's face. " She stands by
our resting-place
And blesses our peaceful love ! "

As she spoke, a flame shot through her breast, and her
eyes of blue
Grew moist with a subtle bliss. " Sweet friend ! " she
cried, and her kiss
Clung soft on the poet's lips.

" Ah, me ! " he sighed, " if they knew, those feverish
lovers who woo

For the passion of tears and blood, how soothing and
　　　　pure and good
　　Is a friendly kiss — like this ! "

"O, list ! " she cried, " 't is a dove ; he calls for his
　　　　absent love ;
They will sit all day and coo calm friendship, like
　　　　mine for you, —
　　Dear friend, like mine for you ! "

Their hands were joined, and a thrill of desire and
　　　　passionate will
Brought his eyes her eyes above in a marvellous look
　　　　of love,
　　And Cupid smiled and drew near.

"O sweetest ! " she whispered softly.　"See ! the god-
　　　　dess is leaning over me,
And smiling with eyes like yours !　O Goddess ! thy
　　　　presence cures
　　The restful unrest of friends ! "

And Cupid laughed in her eyes as he threw off the
white disguise

And bent down to kiss her himself — but cuff! cuff!
on the ears of the elf

From the goddess who sought her robe.

And the river flowed on through the wood, and the
temple of Friendship stood

Like a dream of snow-white stone.   But the minstrel
returned alone

From his pilgrimage.

HER REFRAIN.

"DO you love me?" she said, when the skies were
    blue,
  And we walked where the stream through the
    branches glistened;
And I told and retold her my love was true,
  While she listened and smiled, and smiled and
    listened.

"Do you love me?" she whispered, when days were
    drear,
  And her eyes searched mine with a patient yearning;
And I kissed her, renewing the words so dear,
  While she listened and smiled, as if slowly learning.

"Do you love me?" she asked, when we sat at rest
  By the stream enshadowed with autumn glory;
Her cheek had been laid as in peace on my breast,
  But she raised it to ask for the sweet old story.

And I said: "I will tell her the tale again —
  I will swear by the earth and the stars above me!"
And I told her that uttermost time should prove
The fervor and faith of my perfect love;
And I vowed it and pledged it that nought should
      move;
While she listened and smiled in my face, and then
  She whispered once more, "Do you truly love
      me?"

A SAVAGE.

DIXON, a Choctaw, twenty years of age,
  Had killed a miner in a Leadville brawl;
Tried and condemned, the rough-beards curb their
    rage,
  And watch him stride in freedom from the hall.

" *Return on Friday, to be shot to death !* "
  So ran the sentence — it was Monday night.
The dead man's comrades drew a well-pleased breath;
  Then all night long the gambling dens were bright.

The days sped slowly; but the Friday came,
  And flocked the miners to the shooting-ground;
They chose six riflemen of deadly aim,
  And with low voices sat and lounged around.

" He will not come." " He 's not a fool." " The men
  Who set the savage free must face the blame."
A Choctaw brave smiled bitterly, and then
  Smiled proudly, with raised head, as Dixon came.

Silent and stern — a woman at his heels ;
  He motions to the brave, who stays her tread.
Next minute — flame the guns : the woman reels
  And drops without a moan — Dixon is dead.

LOVE'S SECRET.

L OVE found them sitting in a woodland place,
    His amorous hand amid her golden tresses;
And Love looked smiling on her glowing face
    And moistened eyes upturned to his caresses.

" O sweet," she murmured, " life is utter bliss !"
    " Dear heart," he said, " our golden cup runs over !"
" Drink, love," she cried, " and thank the gods for this !"
    He drained the precious lips of cup and lover.

Love blessed the kiss ; but, ere he wandered thence,
    The mated bosoms heard this benediction :
" *Love lies within the brimming bowl of sense :*
    Who keeps this full has joy — who drains, affliction."

They heard the rustle as he smiling fled :
  She reached her hand to pull the roses blowing.
He stretched to take the purple grapes o'erhead ;
  Love whispered back, " *Nay, keep their beauties grow-*
        ing."

They paused, and understood : one flower alone
  They took and kept, and Love flew smiling over.
Their roses bloomed, their cup went brimming on —
  She looked for Love within, and found her lover.

5

LOVE'S SACRIFICE.

LOVE'S Herald flew o'er all the fields of Greece,
  Crying : " Love's altar waits for sacrifice ! "
And all folk answered, like a wave of peace,
  With treasured offerings and gifts of price.

Toward high Olympus every white road filled
  With pilgrims streaming to the blest abode ;
Each bore rich tribute, some for joys fulfilled,
  And some for blisses lingering on the road.

The pious peasant drives his laden car ;
  The fisher youth bears treasure from the sea ;
A wife brings honey for the sweets that are ;
  A maid brings roses for the sweets to be.

Here strides the soldier with his wreathèd sword,
  No more to glitter in his country's wars ;

There walks the poet with his mystic word,
  And smiles at Eros' mild recruit from Mars.

But midst these bearers of propitious gifts,
  Behold where two, a youth and maiden, stand :
She bears no boon ; his arm no burden lifts,
  Save her dear fingers pressed within his hand.

Their touch ignites the soft delicious fire,
  Whose rays the very altar-flames eclipse ;
Their eyes are on each other — sweet desire
  And yearning passion tremble on their lips.

So fair — so strong !   Ah, Love ! what errant wiles
  Have brought these two so poor and so unblest ?
But see !   Instead of anger, Cupid smiles ;
  And lo ! he crowns their sacrifice as best !

Their hands are empty, but their hearts are filled ;
  Their gifts so rare for all the host suffice :
Before the altar is their life-wine spilled —
  The love they long for is their sacrifice.

A man will trust another man, and show

    His secret thought and act, as if he must;

A woman — does she tell her sins ?   Ah, no !

    She never knew a woman she could trust.

THE WELL'S SECRET.

I KNEW it all my boyhood : in a lonesome valley
    meadow,
  Like a dryad's mirror hidden by the wood's dim
    arches near ;
Its eye flashed back the sunshine, and grew dark and
    sad with shadow ;
  And I loved its truthful depths where every pebble
    lay so clear.

I scooped my hand and drank it, and watched the
    sensate quiver
  Of the rippling rings of silver as the beads of crystal
    fell ;
I pressed the richer grasses from its little trickling river,
  Till at last I knew, as friends know, every secret of
    the well.

But one day I stood beside it on a sudden, unexpected,

   When the sun had crossed the valley and a shadow
      hid the place ;

And I looked in the dark water — saw my pallid cheek
      reflected —

   And beside it, looking upward, met an evil reptile
      face :

Looking upward, furtive, startled at the silent, swift
      intrusion ;

   Then it darted toward the grasses, and I saw not
      where it fled ;

But I knew its eyes were on me, and the old-time
      sweet illusion

   Of the pure and perfect symbol I had cherished
      there was dead.

O, the pain to know the perjury of seeming truth that
      blesses !

   My soul was seared like sin to see the falsehood of
      the place ;

And the innocence that mocked me, while in dim un-
    seen recesses
  There were lurking fouler secrets than the furtive
    reptile face.

And since then, — O, why the burden? — when the
    joyous faces greet me,
  With their eyes of limpid innocence, and words
    devoid of art,
I cannot trust their seeming, but must ask what eyes
    would meet me
  Could I look in sudden silence at the secrets of
    the heart !

JACQUEMINOTS.

I MAY not speak in words, dear, but let my words
    be flowers,
  To tell their crimson secret in leaves of fragrant fire ;
They plead for smiles and kisses as summer fields for
    showers,
  And every purple veinlet thrills with exquisite desire.

O, let me see the glance, dear, the gleam of soft con-
    fession
  You give my amorous roses for the tender hope they
    prove ;
And press their heart-leaves back, love, to drink their
    deeper passion,
  For their sweetest, wildest perfume is the whisper of
    my love !

My roses, tell her, pleading, all the fondness and the
    sighing,
  All the longing of a heart that reaches thirsting for
    its bliss ;
And tell her, tell her, roses, that my lips and eyes are
    dying
  For the melting of her love-look and the rapture of
    her kiss.

Hunger goes sleeplessly
  Thinking of food;
Evil lies painfully
  Yearning for good.
Life is a confluence:
  Nature must move,
Like the heart of a poet,
  Toward beauty and love.

LIVING.

TO toil all day and lie worn-out at night ;
　　To rise for all the years to slave and sleep,
And breed new broods to do no other thing
In toiling, bearing, breeding — life is this
To myriad men, too base for man or brute.

To serve for common duty, while the brain
Is hot with high desire to be distinct ;
To fill the sand-grain place among the stones
That build the social wall in million sameness,
Is life by leave, and death by insignificance.

To live the morbid years, with dripping blood
Of sacrificial labor for a Thought ;
To take the dearest hope and lay it down
Beneath the crushing wheels for love of Freedom ;

To bear the sordid jeers of cant and trade,

And go on hewing for a far ideal, —

This were a life worth giving to a cause,

If cause be found so worth a martyr life.

But highest life of man, nor work nor sacrifice,

But utter seeing of the things that be !

To pass amid the hurrying crowds, and watch

The hungry race for things of vulgar use ;

To mark the growth of baser lines in men ;

To note the bending to a servile rule ;

To know the natural discord called disease

That rots like rust the blood and souls of men ;

To test the wisdoms and philosophies by touch

Of that which is immutable, being clear,

The beam God opens to the poet's brain ;

To see with eyes of pity laboring souls

Strive upward to the Freedom and the Truth,

And still be backward dragged by fear and ignorance ;

To see the beauty of the world, and hear

The rising harmony of growth, whose shade

Of undertone is harmonized decay ;

To know that love is life — that blood is one

And rushes to the union — that the heart

Is like a cup athirst for wine of love ;

Who sees and feels this meaning utterly,

The wrong of law, the right of man, the natural truth,

Partaking not of selfish aims, withholding not

The word that strengthens and the hand that helps ;

Who waits and sympathizes with the pettiest life,

And loves all things, and reaches up to God

With thanks and blessing — he alone is living.

THE CELEBES.

"The sons of God came upon the earth and took wives of the daughters of men." — *Legends of the Talmud.*

DEAR islands of the Orient,
  Where Nature's first of love was spent ;
Sweet hill-tops of the summered land
Where gods and men went hand in hand
In golden days of sinless earth !
Woe rack the womb of time, that bore
The primal evil to its birth !
It came ; the gods were seen no more :
The fields made sacred by their feet,
The flowers they loved, grown all too sweet,
The streams their bright forms mirrorèd,
The fragrant banks that made their bed,

The human hearts round which they wove

Their threads of superhuman love —

These were too dear and desolate

To sink to fallen man's estate ;

The gods who loved them loosed the seas,

Struck free the barriers of the deep,

That rolled in one careering sweep

And filled the land, as 't were a grave,

And left no beauteous remnant, save

Those hill-tops called the Celebes.

WAITING.

HE is coming! he is coming! in my throbbing
  breast I feel it;
There is music in my blood, and it whispers all day long,
That my love unknown comes toward me! Ah, my heart,
  he need not steal it,
For I cannot hide the secret that it murmurs in its song!

O the sweet bursting flowers! how they open, never
  blushing,
  Laying bare their fragrant bosoms to the kisses of the
  sun!
And the birds — I thought 't was poets only read their
  tender gushing,
  But I hear their pleading stories, and I know them every
  one.

" He is coming ! " says my heart ; I may raise my eyes
and greet him ;

I may meet him any moment — shall I know him
when I see ?

And my heart laughs back the answer — I can tell
him when I meet him,

For our eyes will kiss and mingle ere he speaks a
word to me.

O, I 'm longing for his coming — in the dark my arms
outreaching ;

To hasten you, my love, see, I lay my bosom bare !

Ah, the night-wind ! I shudder, and my hands are
raised beseeching —

It wailed so light a death-sigh that passed me in
the air !

6

O, the rare spring flowers! take them as they come:
Do not wait for summer buds — they may never bloom.
Every sweet to-day sends we are wise to save;
Roses bloom for pulling: the path is to the grave.

WHEAT GRAINS.

A S grains from chaff, I sift these worldly rules,
    Kernels of wisdom, from the husks of schools :

I.

Benevolence befits the wisest mind ;

But he who has not studied to be kind,

Who grants for asking, gives without a rule,

Hurts whom he helps, and proves himself a fool.

II.

The wise man is sincere : but he who tries

To be sincere, hap-hazard, is not wise.

III.

Knowledge is gold to him who can discern

That he who loves to know, must love to learn.

IV.

Straightforward speech is very certain good ;
But he who has not learned its rule is rude.

V.

Boldness and firmness, these are virtues each,
Noble in action, excellent in speech.
But who is bold, without considerate skill,
Rashly rebels, and has no law but will ;
While he called firm, illiterate and crass,
With mulish stubbornness obstructs the pass.

VI.

The mean of soul are sure their faults to gloss,
And find a secret gain in others' loss.

VII.

Applause the bold man wins, respect the grave ;
Some, only being *not* modest, think they 're brave.

VIII.

The petty wrong-doer may escape unseen ;

But what from sight the moon eclipsed shall screen ?

Superior minds must err in sight of men,

Their eclipse o'er, they rule the world again.

IX.

Temptation waits for all, and ills will come ;

But some go out and ask the devil home.

X.

" I love God," said the saint.   God spake above :

" Who loveth me must love those whom I love."

" I scourge myself," the hermit cried.   God spake :

" Kindness is prayer ; but not a self-made ache."

THE LURE.

"WHAT bait do you use," said a Saint to the
Devil,

"When you fish where the souls of men abound?"

"Well, for special tastes," said the King of Evil,

"Gold and Fame are the best I 've found."

"But for general use?" asked the Saint. "Ah, then,"

Said the Demon, "I angle for Man, not men,

And a thing I hate

Is to change my bait,

So I fish with a woman the whole year round."

THE EMPTY NICHE.

Read at the farewell reception given to Rev. Robert Fulton, S. J.,
at Boston College Hall, Feb. 5, 1880.

A KING once made a gallery of art,
    With portraits of dead friends and living graced;
And at the end, 'neath curtains drawn apart,
    An empty marble pedestal was placed.

Here, every day, the king would come, and pace
    With eyes well-pleased along the statued hall;
But, ere he left, he turned with saddened face,
    And mused before the curtained pedestal.

And once a courtier asked him why he kept
    The shadowed niche to fill his heart with dole;
"For absent friends," the monarch said, and wept;
    "There still must be one absent to the soul."

And this is true of all the hearts that beat ;
　　Though days be soft and summer pathways fair,
Be sure, while joyous glances round us meet,
　　The curtained crypt and vacant plinth are there.

To-day we stand before our draped recess :
　　There is none absent — all we love are here ;
To-morrow's hands the opening curtains press,
　　And lo, the pallid pediment is bare !

The cold affection that plain duty breeds
　　May see its union severed, and approve ;
But when our bond is touched, it throbs and bleeds —
　　We pay no meed of duty, but of love.

As creeping tendrils shudder from the stone,
　　The vines of love avoid the frigid heart ;
The work men do is not their test alone,
　　The love they win is far the better chart.

They say the citron-tree will never thrive
   Transplanted from the soil where it matured ;
Ah, would 't were so that men could only live
   Through working on where they had love secured !

" The People of the Book," men called the Jews —
   Our priests are truly " People of the Word ; "
And he who serves the Master must not choose —
   He renders feudal service to the Lord.

But we who love and lose will, like the king,
   Still keep the alcove empty in the hall,
And hope, firm-hearted, that some day will bring
   Our absent one to fill his pedestal.

*Soldier, why do you shrink from the hiss of the hungry
    lead?*

* The bullet that whizzed is past : the approaching ball
    is dumb.*

* Stand straight! you cannot shrink from Fate : let it
    come!*

*A comrade in front may hear it whiz — when you are
    dead.*

A SONG FOR THE SOLDIERS.

WHAT song is best for the soldiers?
   Take no heed of the words, nor choose you
      the style of the story ;
Let it burst out from the heart like a spring from the
      womb of a mountain,
Natural, clear, resistless, leaping its way to the levels ;
Whether of love or hate or war or the pathos and pain
      of affliction ;
Whether of manly pluck in the perilous hour, or that
      which is higher,
And highest of all, the slowly bleeding sacrifice,
The giving of life and its joys for the sake of men
      and freedom ; —

Any song for the soldier that will harmonize with the
    life-throbs ;

For he has laved in the mystical sea by which men are
    one ;

His pulse has thrilled into blinding tune with the vaster
    anthems

Which God plays on the battle-fields when He sweeps
    the strings of nations,

And the song of the earth-planet bursts on the silent
    spheres,

Shot through like the cloud of Etna with flames of
    heroic devotion,

And shaded with quivering lines from the mourning of
    women and children !

Here is a song for the soldiers — a song of the Chey-
    enne Indians,

Of men with soldierly hearts who walked with Death
    as a comrade.

Hush ! Let the present fade ; let the distance die ; let
the last year stand :

We are far to the West, in Montana, on the desolate
plains of Montana ;

We ride with the cavalry troopers on the bloody trail
of the Cheyennes,

Forty braves of the tribe who have leaped from the
reservation

Down on the mining camps in their desecrated
valleys,

Down to their fathers' graves and the hunting-ground
of their people.

Chilled with the doom of Death they gaze on the
white men's changes :

Ruthless the brutal force that has crushed their homes
and their manhood,

And ruthless the hearts of the Cheyenne braves as
they swoop on the camps of the miners !

Back to the hills they dash, with reeking trophies
    around them :
But swift on their trail the cavalry ride, and their
    trumpets
Break on the ears of the braves with a threat of on-
    coming vengeance.

At last they are bayed and barred — corralled in a
    straight-walled valley, —
The Indians back to the cliffs with the shattered rocks
    as a breastwork,   .
The soldiers in lined stockades across the mouth of
    the valley.

Hungrily hiss the bullets, not wasted in random firing,
But every shot for a mark, — thrice their number of
    soldiers
Raking the Cheyenne rocks with a pitiless rain of
    missiles,

One to three in the firing, but every Cheyenne bullet
Tumbled a reckless trooper behind his fence in the
stockade.

" God ! they are brave ! " cried the captain. " Seven
hours we 've held them,
Three, ay, five to one, if you count their dead and
their wounded :
Damn them ! why don't they yield for the sake of
their lives and their wounded ? "

•

But never a sign but flame and the hiss of the leaden
defiance
Comes from the Cheyenne braves, though their firing
slackens in vigor
To grow in fatal precision — grim as the cliff above
them
They fight their fight, and the valley is lined with death
from their rifles.

Cried the captain, "Men, we must charge!" and he
      grieves for his boys and their foemen;
"But show them a sign of quarter;" and he swings
      them a flag to tell them
That his side is willing to parley: the Indians riddle
      the ensign,
And the captain groans in his heart as he gives the
      order for charging.
Terrible getting ready of men who prepare for a death-
      fight: —
Scabbards are thrown aside and belts unstrapped for
      the striking,
Ominous outward signs of the deadlier inner pre-
      paring
When the soul flings danger aside and the human heart
      its mercy.

Out from the fatal earthworks, their eyes like fire in a
      cavern,

With naked blades the troopers, and nerves wire-strung
　　for the onset,
When suddenly, up from the rocks, a sign at last from
　　the Cheyennes !

Two tall braves on the rocks — " Re-form ! " brays the
　　cavalry trumpet,
And grimly the soldiers return, reluctantly leaving the
　　conflict.
Still on the rocks two forms of bronze, as if prepared
　　for the stormers,
Then down to the field, and behold, they dash toward
　　the wondering troopers !
The soldiers stare at the charge, but no man laughs
　　at the foemen,
Instead of a sneer a tremor at many a mouth in sorrow.
On they come to their death, and, standing at fifty
　　paces,
They fire in the face of the squadron, and dash with
　　their knives to the death-grip !

7

Fifty rifles give flame, and the breasts of the heroes
    are shattered ;
But falling, they plunge toward the fight, and their
    knives sink deep in the meadow !

" On to the rocks ! " and the soldiers have done with
    their feelings of mercy —
But never a foe to meet them nor a shot from the
    deadly barrier.
First on the rocks the captain, with a cheer that died
    as he gave it, —
A cheer that was half a groan and a cry of admiration.
Awed stood the troopers who followed, and lowered
    their swords with their leader,
Homage of brave to the brave, saluting with souls and
    weapons ;
There at their feet lay the foemen — every man dead
    on his rifle —
The two who had charged the troops were the last
    alive of the Cheyennes !

THE MUTINY OF THE CHAINS.

(PENAL COLONY OF WESTERN AUSTRALIA, 1857.)

THE sun rose o'er dark Fremantle,
 And the Sentry stood on the wall ;
Above him, with white lines swinging,
The flag-staff, bare and tall :
The flag at its foot — the Mutiny Flag —
Was always fast to the line, —
For its sanguine field was a cry of fear,
And the Colony counted an hour a year
In the need of the blood-red sign.

The staff and the line, with its ruddy flash,
Like a threat or an evil-bode,
Were a monstrous whip with a crimson lash,
Fit sign for the penal code.

The Sentry leant on his rifle, and stood
By the mast, with a deep-drawn breath ;
A stern-browed man, but there heaved a sigh
For the sight that greeted his downward eye
In the prison-square beneath.

In yellow garb, in soldier lines,
One hundred men in chains ;
While the watchful warders, sword in hand,
With eyes suspicious keenly scanned
The links of the living lanes.

There, wary eyes met stony eyes,
And stony face met stone.
There was never a gleam of trust or truce ;
In the covert thought of an iron loose,
Grim warder and ward were one.

Why was it so, that there they stood, —
Stern driver and branded slave ?

Why rusted the gyve in the bondman's blood,

No hope for him but the grave?

Out of thousands there why was it so

That one hundred hearts must feel

The bitterest pang of the penal woe,

And the grind of a nation's heel?

Why, but for choice — the bondman's choice?

They balanced the gains and pains ;

They took their chance of the chains.

There spake in their hearts a hidden voice

Of the blinding joy of a freeman's burst

Through the great dim woods.   Then the toil accurst ;

The scorching days and the nights in tears ·

The riveted rings for years and years ;

They weighed them all — they looked before

At the one and other, and spoke them o'er,

And they saw what the heart of man must see,

That the uttermost blessing is Liberty !

Ah, pity them, God ! they must always choose,

For the life to gain and the death to lose.

They dream of the woods and the mountain spring,

And they grasp the flower, to clutch the sting.

Even so : they are better than those who bend

Like beasts to the lash, and go on to the end

As a beast will go, with to-day for a life,

And to-morrow a blank.   Offer peace and strife

To a man enslaved — let him vote for ease

And coward labor, and be content ;

Or let him go out in the front, as these,

With their eyes on the doom and the danger, went.

And take your choice — the man who remains

A self-willed serf, or the one who stains

His sudden hand with a drive for light

Through a bristling rank and a gloomy night.

This man for me — for his heart he 'll share

With a friend : with a foe, he 'll fight him fair.

And such as he are in every rank

Of the column that moves with a dismal clank

And a dead-march step toward the rock-bound place

Where the chain-gangs toil — o'er the beetling face

Of the cliff that roots in the Swan's deep tide :

Steep walls of granite on either side,

At the precipice' foot the river wide ;

Behind them in ranks the warders fall ;

And above them, the Sentry paces the wall.

Year in, year out, has the Sentry stood

On the wall at the foot of the mast.

He has turned from the toilers to watch the flood

Like his own slow life go past.

He has noted the Chains grow fat and lean ;

He has sighed for their empty spaces,

And thought of the cells where their end had been,

Where they lay with their poor dead faces,

With never a kiss, or prayer, or knell —

They were better at rest in the river ;

He thinks of the shadow that o 'er them fell
From the mast with its whip-like quiver ;
He has seen it tipped with its crimson lash
When the mutiny-flood had risen
And swept like a sea with an awful swash
Through the squares and the vaulted prison.
His thoughts are afar with the woful day,
With the ranged dead men and the dying,
And slowly he treads till they pass away ——

Then a pause, and a start, and a scuffling sound,
And a glance beneath, at a battle-ground,
Where the lines are drawn, and the Chains are found
Their armèd guards defying !
A hush of death — and the Sentry stands
By the mast, with the halyards tight in his hands,
And the Mutiny Flag is flying !

Woe to the weak, to the mutineers !
The bolt of their death is driven ;

A mercy waits on all other tears,

But the Chains are never forgiven.

Woe to the rebels ! — their hands are bare,

Their manacled bodies helpless there ;

Their faces lit with a strange wild light,

As if they had fought and had won the fight !

No cry is uttered — upraised no hand ;

All stilled to a muscle's quiver ;

One line on the brink of the cliff they stand,

Their shadows flung down on the river.

The quarry wall is on either side,

The blood-red flag high o'er them ;

But the lurid light in their eyes defied

The gathering guards before them.

No parley is held when the Chains revolt :

Grimly silent they stand secure

On the outward lip of the embrasure ;

Waiting fierce-eyed for the fatal bolt.

A voice from the guard, in a monotone ;

A voice that was cold and hard as stone : —
" Make ready !   Fire ! "
                              O Christ, the cry
From the manacled men ! not fear to die,
Or whine for mercy ; rebelled they stood,
Well knowing the price of revolt was blood ;
Well knowing — but each one knew that he
Would sell his blood for his liberty !

Unwarned by a word, uncalled, unshriven,
They dare by a look — and the doom is given.
They raise their brows in the wild revolt,
And God's wrath flames in the fierce death-bolt ;
God's wrath ? — nay, man's ; God never smote
A rebel dead whose swelling throat
Was full with protest.   Hear, then smite ;
God's justice weighs not shrieks the right.

"Make ready !   Fire ! "
                              Again outburst
The horror and shame for the deed accurst !

O, cry of the weak, as the hot blood calls

From the burning wound, and the stricken falls

With his face in the dust ; and the strong one stands,

With scornful lips and ensanguined hands ;

O, blood of the weak, unbought, unpriced,

Thy smoke is a piteous prayer to Christ !

They stand on the brink of the cliff — they bend

To the dead in their chains ; then rise, and send

To the murdering muzzles defiant eyes.

" Make ready !   Fire ! "

                The smoke-clouds rise :

They are still on the face of the cliff — they bend

Once more to the dead — they whisper a word

To the hearts in the dust — then, undeterred,

They raise their faces, so grimly set,

Till the eyes of slayer and doomed have met.

O merciful God, let thy pity rain

Ere the hideous lightning leaps again !

They have sinned — they have erred — let the living

       stand —

They have dared and rued — let thy loving hand

Be laid on those brows that bravely face

The death that shall wash them of all disgrace !

Be swift with pity — O, late, too late !

The tubes are levelled — the marksmen wait

For the word of doom — the spring is pressed

By the nervous finger — the sight is straight —

" Make ready ! " —

              Why falters the dread command ?

Why stare as affrighted the armèd band ?

Why lower the rifles from shoulder to hip,

Why dies the word on the leader's lip,

While the voice that was hard grows husky deep,

And the face is a-tremble as if to weep ?

The Chains on the brink of the cliff are lined ;

The living are bowed o 'er the dead — they rise

And they face the rifles with burning eyes ;

Then they bend again, and with one set mind

They raise the dead and the wounded raise

In their loving arms with words of praise

And tender grief for the torturing wounds.

One backward step with a burdened tread —

They bear toward the precipice wounded and dead —

Then they turned on the cliff to front the guard

With faces like men that have died in fight ;

Their brows were raised as if proud reward

Were theirs, and their eyes had a victor's light.

They spoke not a word, but stood sublime

In their sombre strength, and the watchers saw

That they smiled as they looked, and their words were
       heard

As they spoke to the dying a loving word.

They were Men at last — they knew naught of crime ;

They were masters and makers of life and law.

They turned from the guard that quailed and shrank

From the gleaming eyes of the burdened rank ;

They turned on the cliff, and a sob was heard

As they looked far down on the darkened river ;

They raised their eyes to the sky — they grasped

The dead to their breasts, while the wounded clasped

The necks of the brothers who bore their weight —

Then they sprang from the cliff, as a horse will spring

For his life from a precipice — sprang to death

In silence and sternness — one deep breath,

As they plunged, of liberty, thrilled their souls,

And then — the Chains were at rest forever !

University Press : John Wilson & Son, Cambridge.

www.ingramcontent.com/pod-product-compliance
Lightning Source LLC
Chambersburg PA
CBHW030544270326
41927CB00008B/1508